The State of the World(And My Mind Have Much In Common)

Jeya Mackelle

BookLeaf Publishing

India | USA | UK

Presentation by *BookLeaf Publishing*

Web: www.bookleafpub.com

E-mail: info@bookleafpub.com

ISBN: 9789357214681

First edition 2022

ACKNOWLEDGEMENT

I'd like to give my thanks to Bookleaf Publishing for presenting me with this golden opportunity and helping me to further my writing career. Every person on this team, from one side of the globe to the other is amazing and incredible, and I can never express my gratitude enough.
Thank you so very much!

Colored World

I am the crimson of a thousand nations' pasts,
The yellow of the rising sun in our lands.
Standing on the green of a country united for all,
Shedding blue tears of joy and sorrow.
And dancing in the purple rain of tomorrow's
end.
The silver of the past taints the present,
But it is in my power to paint the future gold.
Stand in solidarity with all the world's colors.
Or fall down with the rest in the gray.

Riding Time's Wavelength

If tomorrow was but a ship in the distance,
I would be a speedboat, catching up in a
moment.
If a year from now I knew I was going to die,
I'd wait an extra day to tell everyone.
If yesterday I had said what I will tomorrow,
Maybe I could save you all yet.
But a century has passed without my knowledge.
Now I am weary of this world and its trivialities.
So on the ship I must go, sailing to another era.

The First Season of Love

Spring, my first love,
Delicate like the flowers of early morning.
Full of hope as the sun's rays at dawn,
As pure as the first drop of golden dew.
It brushes its cool fingers across my cheek,
Whispering of precious treasures yet to be.
I wrap myself in the colors—pink, blue, yellow.
Each one, special and reminiscent of a time not
so long ago.
Spring, young and vibrant, reminds me of you.

Life in Eleven Seconds

Count to ten with me—
One white rose for your eternal promise.
Two pairs of feet walking side by side.
Three fingers on the edge of my cheek.
Four claps for a single line on a stick.
Five screams for the fear of two.
Six tears I shed for the day to come.
Seven decades of peace, seven days of sorrow.
Eight hands held together in solidarity.
Nine smiles gathered around us.
And ten seconds to bid you goodbye.
Eleven before I join you.

Divine Destruction

Forging a new path amid the leaves,
Kicking up the dust of a crumbled city.
Gazing around at the dreary landscape,
I remember: I escaped!
Once long ago, running away.
I fled from the decay and ruin,
Toward a sanctuary only found in dreams.
Where I was alone but safe and happy.
Now, looking out over the fallen metropolis,
Seeing the error of my ways, I know:
Destruction and chaos are at my own hand.
And I am their creator, mortal and infinite.

May the Flames of Hope Forever Burn

See there the pain of several billion souls,
Lined up like lanterns, glowing an eerie green.
Malice and contempt rest on heavy shoulders,
Worn down by years of discord and struggle.
Who will bear the torch and save us, they cry.
Who will release us from the decay of a
civilization?
I stand tall, holding the golden flame in hand,
Its light bright as the angry sun,
And with it, all the world is at my command.

Time is Not A Thief(He's a Procrastinator)

Churning away at each second, the Master of
Time,
Sits every minute, wasting yours and mine.
He ponders the meaning of life by the hour,
In the night, in the morning, whilst taking his
shower.
For Time, that's fine and dandy and all.
But for me, it causes quite a bit of trouble.
Now I know this one thing for sure.
Time is not a thief, but a procrastinator.

Dreamcatcher

A million people crossing the street,
Each one couldn't care less about me.
Not realizing I am capturing their faces,
To store in a hundred random places.
They don't know you and they don't know me.
Yet we always find each other repeatedly.
Sitting under the same canopy with one another,
Stuck together in my elaborate dreamcatcher.
You've never met me and you probably never
will.
But in my dreams you and I die on the same hill.

A Generation's Blight

Bullets, they rain down upon us,
Like acid from a toxic sky.
With them comes the words passed down to an
innocent generation.
Trash, filth, worthless, drain on society.
These words do not define me.
I will yell back louder than the ruckus.
I won't stop to ask them why.
They will be repelled by the voice of a hundred
nations.
Invisible shields blocking out your hatred,
And flooding the streets with a new hope.

The World's A Stage(Which I Shall Consume)

I'm just a scavenger of worlds,
Traveling there and here.
Collecting stardust from each atmosphere.
I take pieces of each planet with me,
Locking them in a box hidden the galaxy.
Pluto, Mars, and Venus all know me by name.
Soon, your world will be mine, just the same.
A black hole, sucking up all within her sight,
Your existence wiped away, stolen from the
light.

Out of the Light, Into the Dark

A hundred trillion lights glowing prettily,
Yet I sit here in the dark, smiling sadly.
A world full of billions, always talking.
But when I speak, no one's really listening.
Realistically, I can't keep doing this, hiding.
My mind, however, keeps on deciding for me.
"We're not going to do it today. Not yet."
Then when will we be able to come out?
Is there ever a good time to expose yourself,
Or are you destined to live and die in the
darkness?
Let us go together, burdened by these lights no
more.
Succumb to the dark and spend your nights with
me.

Happy New Year!

January.
New beginnings and hopes.
A new reason, perhaps, to cope.
Smile at the year's first dawn,
And arise, to be this year's new pawn.
June.
Halfway through the dreary year.
Your mind is alive, harvesting new fears.
You push on, that smile starts to slip.
On your shoulder is a brand new chip.
December.
This was a special kind of year.
One that brought new aches and old tears.
You're bored right now at the party, drained.
Every day makes you a little more insane.
You're done, ready to go to sleep and wake,
To another year; oh for goodness sake!
January.

Decem Verbum

I learned ten new words today.
Defenestrate: what I want to do to my boss.
Eudaimonia: a break from the chaos.
Komorebi: just a glimpse to last a lifetime.
Limerence: I felt this at one moment in time.
Meraki: I hope someone will find it one day.
Numinous: it's right there, not too far away.
Hiraeth: I've been there a thousand times in my
dreams.
Aliferous: oh to fly, oh to be one of those with
wings.
Ethereal: you when you talk and I begin to
daydream.
Apathetic: that's how I feel after reading, it
seems.

Heaven and Hell Next Door

If Heaven were a place,
An ethereal space.
I would visit everyday,
Leaving my life far away.
If "going to hell" was possible,
I make it there and back, no trouble.
I nod and bow to the two Angels below and
above,
Bask in their deep and unfiltered Love.
If Heaven and Hell were just next door,
That's where you'd find me, on the 4th floor.

Reality: Ultimate Simulation Game

Breaking through reality and the atmosphere,
I've finally figured everything out.
We're living in the ultimate simulation.
Heading towards a life of self-destruction.
It's all one, big, made-up infection.
There will be no resurrection.
I'm waiting for the insurrection.
This time, there will be no intervention.
This dying world is of our own invention.
What's the point of mortal retention?
As I said, we are past the point of redemption.
Human beings rarely ever learn their lesson.
Abandon your worldly possessions.
Now I'll sit and wait for the pain to lessen,
Here in my self-prescribed detention.

Fernweh

There is a place out there that I know.
Somewhere so pristine and peaceful.
Nowhere else that I'd ever be caught.
Surpassing its beauty, Heaven could not.
Forgetting where I came from, abandoning my
roots.
Passing eternity living in my pretty version of
truth.
I want to stay here in this place forever,
Never going back to how things were.
I've never been there, but I remember it well.

H.O.U.S.E.

Huddled by an inviting fire, kept warm by love.
Overwhelmed by security and surrounded by
family.
Unbelieving of where you are, yet aware of
others less lucky.
Scattered memories of loved ones and peace,
Entangled with the days of uncertainty and
hopelessness.
Be grateful in this moment for all you own,
And never boast for you will lose it all and be
forever alone.

Memories of a Winter Blue

Breathing in the crisp winter air,
But wishing for the quick arrival of spring.
Creating snow angels on the ground,
Your only chance at ever having wings.
You throw a snowball at your friend's face;
You missed, but it's all in good fun.
Later, sipping rich cocoa by the fire,
A part of you wishes it could all just be done.
Edgar Allen Poe on a frostbitten night,
Reminds you of your old home.
Of forgotten joy, distant memories, misplaced
moments.
It all comes back to remind you of that first cold
day in winter.

Live Young, Die Free

Never allow yourself to forget.
Live loud, live free, and without shame.
No one can stop you; it's all your choice.
Remain in that far-away valley, safe and sound.
Migrate to a city, a bright, flashy world,
Full of so many visions and memories.
You can have your cake and eat it too.
Never let anyone tell you that you can't.
My world is your oyster, my dream to share.
It's not up to them—it's up to me.

How To Write A Poem

Sit in your blue chair, pen in hand, fingers on the
keyboard.
Stare into the empty space—wait for ideas to
come.
Imagine all the opportunities you have in store.
Ponder silently. You want something deep, but
not too fun.
Tap your fingers against the desk and heave a
sigh.
Frustration has never had such a hold on you.
Wait for hours for one tiny spark to get you high.
Just write those words. Doesn't matter if they're
true.

Post-Quarantine, 20...?

After the Quarantine, what else is there?
When the pain and fire has subsided,
And we all come out of hiding,
Who's going to start the Revolution?
Which of us will lead the new generation?
Once the government is dead,
There sits our leader's head,
Who will be the one to dare?
Quarantine is over, what's next?